WINGS BORN
from a
HARVEST OF THORNS

WINGS BORN
from a
HARVEST OF THORNS

The **Haneef R Jordan** Story

HANEEF R JORDAN

Library of Congress Control Number: 2018906910

ISBN: 978-1-7323-0581-6

T here are moments in life that define us. This story I will share here is one of those moments when the Master's hand began mysteriously shaping me into the vessel that I was predestined to become.

I will start my journey at the very beginning. I would like to offer you a keyhole peek into a past that has mostly being locked behind a door marked "Private" and "Do Not Enter." I will allow you to meet a younger version of myself. I will allow you to meet the child in me who was so vulnerable and innocent to the plans that life had in store for me. Life is like a sly dealer shuffling cards to chance and serving one a hand that they cannot refuse. On this day that my story starts I was like a young diamond in the making. All diamonds begin as ordinary chunks of dark coal. It is only under great heat and pressure and over time that a metamorphosis occurs. I was as yet this simple dark coal. Life was simple then. I was fourteen. I did what children do. I went to school. I played with my friends and I trusted my mother. That was all to change.

There was nothing particularly special about the man my mother brought home that day. I was neither impressed nor dismayed by him at first. If our intuition is our internal voice, mine was immediately on the phone making an emergency call to my brain. The message I received was that I did not like this stranger who would change the entire course of my life. His would be the heavy baggage that I would carry with me for my lifetime until the day when I empowered myself to do what we all must do with trash...dispose of it.

On this day the dealer called happenstance was what appeared to be a casual introduction to my mother's new boyfriend. But within moments I realized that she was in fact introducing me to her new husband. Trust is like a fragile glass vase and once shattered it often times can never be repaired perfectly, and it retains the outward blemishes of the damage that occurred. Such was this moment. My mother, a beautiful, strong woman, was now suddenly the impulsive stranger announcing a new husband whom we had never heard about before.

This was the Club of Spades I had just been dealt, and soon it would be digging us all into a hole of dark despair that would take forever to escape.

"He is a liar Mommy, please be careful. I just don't trust him. I don't know why but there is something about him..."

"Hush child! Don't talk to me like I'm one of your friends. I am a grown woman! This is my man and you are a child! I will not discuss my private affairs with a child. Now please be respectful of me and my decision and your new stepfather."

I remember the fireplace was spitting flames with the same vengeance that life was about to shoot me with painful arrows. It was a cold night and neither the warmth of the fire nor the womb of my bed could bring me the warmth and peace of mind I desired. In retrospect I would say that this moment marked the murdering of my innocence. I was a premature infant born to a harsh world before my ripe time. I did not know it but the fanciful days of my childhood were departing swiftly from me like wild horses escaping a pending storm. A dark time was upon us.

I did not go to school that day. I was a prisoner to my mother's fear. She told me in stifled whispers that she feared for her life. I did not know what to do with this information so I did what we all do, I opened an invisible bag and started loading it up with what would become my emotional baggage.

Some memories are like pieces of papers with scribbles of images, sounds, smells and other such sensations in which we store the past. This particular piece of paper is one that I've crumbled a million times and tried to throw away. Finally with every word that I write, I am blessed to feel the wings of hope begin to take shape and with an open heart sad things must fly away and set me free.

As with most patterns of abuse, the sounds of arguing which I listened to all through the night were blaring red flags. My mother eventually found the strength and composure to leave for work. But unfortunately she was leaving me with her monster. The beast looked like a man but he was not equipped with the ability to make moral judgments or distinguish right from wrong. This beast of a man had roamed the cold and dark cave of my mother's bedroom all night growling out into the night like a fiend. At least the hours of darkness had kept me safe. Now, he was my dragon to slay. The fire-breathing beast of a man must not have consumed enough rage fighting with my mother because now he slithered from the shadows like a hellbound soul salivating to eat something young and deliciously innocent.

Demons have faces like human men sometimes. In fact the devil could manifest himself on two legs like a man with trunks of arms and a giant's fists. I cannot recall the inciting incidents. All I know is that words can be fire starters. No sooner had my words left my mouth they had burned a path into the ears of a heartless man. They say words are like hands; they never come back empty handed. Well my words must have been soldiers, because when I sent them forth it was to fight a war I could not win. Only a weak and pathetic man cannot defend himself against the words of a child with words. This beast decided that the only way to stop the surge of words marching out of my mouth was to shut my mouth with the brute force of a giant closed fist and its rocks of knuckles. This was the instance I lost a piece of myself like a rose dropping petals. I remember nothing. I only remember the impact of a fist, ringing in my ears and the welcome blanket of darkness pulling me to safety.

When I opened my eyes I was laying on the floor. My broken heart, my trust and my happiness were all beaten to the ground.

I looked up and the creature was standing over me. A possessed smile lurked on his big face. I know that wrath is one of the seven deadly sins, but in that moment I succumbed to it. How dare this thing hit me and then take such great pleasure in it! I will pause here to draw your attention to my earlier analogy of how life is a hand that shapes us. In this second unbeknownst to me the master was shaping the clay which was laying hurt and disgraced on the floor. In that harshly expelled breath with the acidic taste of blood flooding my mouth, I did not see the seed of greatness that had been planted in me. From this moment I would never be this child again. From this moment I was becoming the woman who would have the ability to overcome insurmountable challenges in life to make her dreams come true. Indeed, the devil is a liar because what that man and I could not see was that I was not lying on the floor, defeated. Nor was he the victor towering over me. On the contrary, he was the pathetic spirit of a small man with a smaller ego and a cripple of morality spiritually sprawled out, defeated by life. He was the loser. I was in fact the tall, proud, strong spirit of a great lady in the making, towering mountains over him, and victorious. How much smaller the speck of dust, which is now my memory of him, appears in the rear view mirror of my life. Now the moments that he stole from me are the secret flames of my passion and determination to be a resounding success in this life and to leave a great legacy of hope.

I have other pieces of paper in the pocket of my imagination. On those pieces I see the collage of scrambled puzzle pieces of images from the past. Fists. My mom lying on the floor. Me scrambling to help her. The blue and red lights of police sirens. Voices over speakers. The blur of the TV playing in the background. As I write these words I would like to finally crumble all these pieces of papers and throw them away. I have finally opened up my heavy baggage and I am unpacking my sordid past so that I can walk into my present blessings.

Tears. I remember a lot of tears. That was the glue in those days that I used to bind my fear, rage and hate to my heart.

From that day on I hated men!

"F-men & F the world!"

Obviously those thoughts would manifest themselves in my future. Be careful what you think because it becomes your destiny. By sixteen years I ran away from my childhood home to the far more empathetic streets. The streets were real. The streets were predictable. The streets were the bridge that I now had to cross in search of a better life. I did not ponder it much in that space, but undeniably I was filled with a hope that was more powerful than all the disappointment and hurt in me. It was hope that propelled me forward. My anger kept the home fires burning.

The streets are full of life changing lessons, wisdom and shadows. They say be watchful who you entertain, as you might entertain angels disguised as beggars. The drug-dealing boy, who was my first oracle, told me that I was on the streets but not of the streets. He was the first of many life mentors. There was nothing but truth to his words and so they found a fertile ground in my spirit and began to fill me with growing hope.

I started the miraculous juggling act of putting myself through school, working and trying to find a place to live. I was technically homeless, but it was yet another lesson in trusting in things not seen and not falling prisoner to the cage of circumstances. Although things appeared bleak, I could see my dreams because I was the light that illuminated my path. In those early days as a sixteen-year-old girl I could not see myself as the light. I was too busy looking for something that was already inside of me.

We will talk in later chapters about the journey of finding the things that were never to be searched for. Of all the gifts that God gave us, the one that we must pray for first is the gift of sight. With open eyes we see the opportunity and abilities that are always part of us. Without sight, we spend a lifetime looking for things that do not and cannot live outside of our hearts, spirits and souls. The things of my past had left scars on my heart but my spirit was not broken and my soul was untouched.

Let us close this door and peek into yet another keyhole at a different time in my life. I was now a young woman of 22. I was young in years, but I was an old soul by virtue of the things that I had seen.

When we are not whole and when we still need healing we become very weary because it is not love that brings us to this fragile state.

Broken people attract other broken people in a futile effort to complete each other. This only leads to co-dependency, which is another slippery slope to an abusive relationship. Many roads lead to abuse.

When I met my handsome, hardworking boyfriend with no apparent baby daddy baggage he became my instant hero. That was my first mistake. The real hero... myself... was once again put on the back burner of my mind and my expectation were unduly placed on love.

Young girls are often easy to woo with fervent promises and physical passion. When there is a father figure void in one's life, this space is like a precious safe full of the most precious things without a lock. Any thief can enter. And so it came to pass. I let my guard down eager to find the connection that would bring me love and happiness. Soon the young man had moved in with me and we were dating.

Imagine a sudden violent hurricane brewing on the horizon of an otherwise sunny day and raging over everything in its way. That is how capriciously I went from the bliss of being in love to been screamed at:

"BITCH! I ain't going nowhere!"

Everything changed me. In slow motion I saw the all too familiar fight posture of a fist flying through the air to knock my faith and breath out of my body. I flew back crashing into the couch behind me.

Time stood still. I was walking around all the corpses of myself laying hurting in every past abuse.

Why me? What was I doing wrong to keep reliving this hell? How had I turned into the mother I so deeply resented and recreated her abusive relationship in my own?

I prayed for it to be a quarter past this very next breath.

Time continued. Blood gushing and a scream. I had had enough. I had formed a fist of my own and hit him with so much force as to try to bring pain to every single person who had ever hurt me. I was tilting at windmills. I was fighting shadows, past monsters and yet another normal seeming person who had shape shifted into an all too familiar monster. I was turning into one myself!

"You stupid bitch you made me bleed!"

Funny, I thought, how he felt that I should care. Strange how monsters can't see themselves and perplexing how monsters don't want to encounter monsters.

Sex was the magic wand that put together this Humpty Dumpty of a love affair when fists tore it asunder. Sex was a bandage for the love that was missing. But 2 years later I was tired of wearing masks and I wanted the wound to heal. Playing out the familiar ritualistic dance of police escorts, fear and restraining orders, I took my power back.

But it would not be that easy to purge myself of monsters.

It was a brief calm before another storm.

I heard this loud BOOM!

The shower door was flung open and he pulled me out by my hair. He hit me repeatedly in the face. It took me a moment to recognize my attacker. As my head was being slammed into the bathroom sink I cried out to God.

"Lord if you get me through this I will do better with my life!"

I was tired of playing the victim in a reoccurring script with just the lead monsters changing. A beating is surreal. I was watching myself getting beaten: present yet disconnected. He grabbed my hair and dragged me into the living room. He climbed on me and started choking me. I fought back which only enraged him further. The loving boyfriend was gone and in his place was this red-eyed hot-tempered dragon picking me up as effortlessly as picking up a child and throwing me across the room.

Silence.

I lay on the floor in the shattered glass, my body aching.

"BITCH if you ever try to leave me again I will kill you!"

He walked to the front door with thundering footsteps. My reality was a distorted compilation of dizzy walls, door slamming shut, excruciating pain, and breathing. I was beyond crying. I crawled to my bedroom yanking off my battered sun dress. I crawled to the living room and to the phone. Some voices in my head blaming myself. I wondered why I was so needy. I asked myself what was wrong with me. I didn't know what I would tell the police.

The broken little girl who had braved the streets to escape an abusive home had run only long and far enough to conjure up the same tragic picture with the all too familiar monster. The broken little girl had grown up into a broken young woman and this hurting young woman had finally had enough.

The accusatory voices in my head were all wrong. It was this dangerous pattern of unconscious thoughts born out of childhood abuse and a lack of positive words of affirmation from a parent which had co-created this reality. And even as I struggled with what my next actions should be, I looked at my demons dead in the eyes and I became David knocking down the Goliath of my fear.

"Honey, if you don't press charges he will do it again." The officer on the other end of the call was a much-needed voice of encouragement and sound reason.

Like a weak, small brand new lion cub looking to walk for the first time but buckling over on fragile legs: such is the herculean efforts of daring faith and courage to take a stand. I had failed so many times before, but my unwavering determination to keep trying and to acquire a new and better life was the secret power that I didn't know I possessed. Looking back, these would be the hallmarks of my journey and the magic ingredients to all success.

It took many years to forgive myself for what I had allowed in my life. That moment was the last and heaviest piece of luggage that I had packed away in my emotional baggage, after the day of my first beating so many years ago. I had encountered so many monsters that somehow I began to think that I was inviting them into my life. I felt as if I was weak and had allowed these tragedies, forgetting that what had happened to me was not a physical war to be conquered by brute force. The war that had raged on me was spiritual, emotional, psychological, mental and metaphysical, and I had in fact been my own hero and a formidable opponent for the devil!

Once again, let me call close attention to my state of thinking, because my self-blaming jail of thoughts was the most dangerous force in my life, long after the monsters were vanquished. My thoughts were the last and most powerful monster that I now had to overcome.

Trying to understand why I could not have seen the signs of an abuser in my own life with the clarity which I had seen it in my mother's life was vexing to me. Yet it would be like standing close to the trunk of a tree then wondering why you didn't see the whole forest. To call upon that gift of sight I touched upon before, it is usually the things that are hiding in plain sight that are the most difficult to see. And hindsight is always superior.

I will pause here for a while with my story. I will gladly close these open doors, for they and the monsters that they hold can no longer haunt me. As a little girl, the monsters lived under my bed; then as a young woman the monsters lived in my bed. Now I wanted to live without them. The voices in my head that had whispered lies of my responsibility to affect the sick behavior of the criminally insane have been overridden by the peace of God that passes all understanding. The master's hands have curved the masterpiece, which is Haneef Jordan. The seeds of hope, perseverance, and determination that were planted into a broken vessel are now the bountiful harvest that is coming into its rightful season. My tears watered all these wonderful things in all the many places where life tried to bury them alive. As for what the future holds? Well you will have to join me again on my adventures in my full autobiography to come!

The phone rang thrice before I answered. At first I did not recognize the voice on the other end nor did I comprehend the words that were spoken.

"Please don't hang up."

How did this old monster get my number and what did he want!

Silence.

"My life has changed for the better. I am now married with 3 kids. When you put me in jail I had to deal with what I had done to you. I got help. I hope you will one day forgive me for all the damage I caused in your life."

All monsters see only the damage they have done but they are blind to see how God uses even these painful, violent, senseless things to turn dark coal into a perfect, precious, priceless diamond.

This time the dealer dealt me the Joker and the joke was not on me!

"I hope you will forgive me one day."

Forgiveness would not be for any monster but for myself, because I was no longer lugging around other people's emotional baggage. Forgiveness would make my load in life lighter. Would you forgive? I know I will never forget.

But today is a brand new day. It is mine to do with as I please. I have my gifts and life as a blessing and my success is finally in the right hero's hands - my own.

I sat back, still in shock from the brief call. I never answered the ghost from the past. I just hung up my phone. The past no longer had power over me.

I grabbed my "Simply Haneef" brand signature coffee cup. I had a radio guest calling in shortly. I was living my dream and building my million-dollar brand. I was surrounded by love from family and true friends. I was finally free of monsters. Now they were forever confined shamefully to the pages of my book.

I am Simply Haneef, and this is my life story.

Finally, that dealer called life has dealt me my best card & truest card ... the Queen of Hearts!

www.ingramcontent.com/pod-product-compliance
Lightning Source LLC
Chambersburg PA
CBHW060550030426
42337CB00021B/4520